DOWNLOADS FROM ONE CONSCIOUSNESS

A PERSONAL JOURNEY TO ENLIGHTENMENT

MONALISA COBURN

PennyByte Books

Downloads from One Consciousness
A Personal Journey to Enlightenment

Published by PennyByte Books
an imprint of PennyByte Publishers
PO Box 1 Rail Road Flat, CA 95248

www.pennybytebooks.com

Cover astrophotography "Alnitak Glory"
by Charles H.Coburn

Paperback ISBN: 978-0-9616594-5-5

10 9 8 7 6 5 4 3

DEDICATION

Dedicated with great gratitude to the ONE CONCIOUSNESS!

Now and now and now...

TABLE OF CONTENTS

ACKNOWLEDGMENTS

Charles Coburn for his endless support.
Naomi Alver McAlpin for being my hero.
My inner being, spirit guides, Yeshua, Mother Mary, and more for without them this book would not have been possible.

Prologue

This inspirational read was written without plan or forethought. It came to me one day at a time after or during a visit from the spiritual world which I'm learning is *this* world. These are personal experiences of awakening that involve my Great Grandfather Yeshua, Jesus Christ.

Please note that my awakening journey began very slowly many years ago. I have always had some psychic abilities like astral projecting, and having out of body experiences, even in my youth. After going to a public four-year college, I learned pretty much that God was a lie and we all came from apes. I became disillusioned and struggled with my faith.

What is our purpose if we just turn to dust? In my mid-thirties, my sister Toodie passed away causing much grief for me. Then her visits from the other side let me know we *do* continue after death. At that point I felt all those who believed otherwise just weren't "in the know."

A few years later, Dr. Wayne Dyer in 2000 introduced me to the concept that we are spiritual beings living in a human body and I've been on my own spiritual journey ever since. During that time, I wrote a series of novels called Dream Navigators that I feel was inspired from my dreams, my spirit guides, and life on the other side. I will continue to work to see that they are published for all to read soon.

With this book, these writings occurred within one month's time. I have journaled this month's spiritual experiences hoping that they may inspire you on your own personal spiritual path. May it be a light... a seed... inspiration to those who are willing to let the glass shatter.

With abundant love and gratitude, MonaLisa Coburn

Download  1
YESHUA ON SHATTERING GLASS WALLS
June 5

Dearest Grandfather, Yeshua, Jesus Christ, and all the other names that have been given you:

First, how are you?

> *"I'm fine. Thank you, my dearest Granddaughter.*
> *Yes, you hear me laughing. You look older than I*
> *at this time. Don't worry... Granddaughter,*
> *Grandfather are labels of the Earth realm."*

"My question is this: I'm getting questions about you from others that know me. How do I answer them honestly without shattering their glass walls so-to-speak."

> *Always answer them with the truth. Tell them it's*
> *the truth that has been revealed to you and the*
> *truth as you see it. Tell them too that we share a*
> *unique bond in that you can channel what is*
> *known as the Yeshua Consciousness through*
> *your writing. It is part of your gifts. Secondly, we*
> *all know what happens to glass when you drop it.*
> *Sometimes walls need to crumble.*

"So a friend of mine asked, "When are you coming back?" I wanted to tell them that you are here. That you *are* back, but I didn't say a word."

> *"You would have been correct as love*
> *consciousness for those who have ears to hear,*
> *eyes to see. Remember when you saw me with*
> *your third eye?"*

"Yes, you had a beautiful golden glow. I felt so fortunate to see you and feel your love. So I say, my grandfather Yeshua has come back, and is here for all those who know that God is within. We are souls with human bodies, and we have an open heart, love, and willing to stay still, as in quiet long enough to invite you to us?"

> *See... not magical, not magical at all. Not even superhuman power unless you call love superhuman power. Love is the strongest magical, superhuman power of all. Never forget my child, never forget love.*

"Yes, well. I've been working on love my entire life. I do love animals unconditionally, my children, my family, friends, but... and then there's that but. I know you taught us not to judge others, least we be judged, but..."

> *Unconditional love has no buts Unconditional means without conditions. Also it helps to have self-love that is unconditional. And that, my child, is the one area that you are working on. I see your glow, your beautiful glow. You are hard, very hard on yourself. Let me give you a gift. God, source within, loves you without conditions. Like in your writings you often say, "You are perfect in your imperfections." You are loved, you are love, and shall always be. There is no larger truth than that.*

"I feel the truth in your words. I wish how you are talking to me now, that you could talk to me when I need you and when others need me."

> *You can! Try it! We are always here. WE being love, spirit guides, angels, and so much more.*

> *Will you be there?*

"You say it like it's so easy. Why do I have a hard time hearing you at times? At other times like this, it's easy and you come in clear... Oh, Law of Attraction!"

"Yes, one law of the universe. Do you remember others?"

"One law is…Law of One: The one is the all, the all is the one."

"Law number two is that we are, so we shall always be…we're eternal."

"Law three is the law of attraction."

"Law number four is that the only constant is change. I do believe there is one more."

"What do they mean to you?"

"One is all and all is the one, says God is all and all is God. The rock, the flower, the animals, the beggar, the king, the universe."

"Number two: We exist, so we shall always exist. We have no end. Our physical body may end, but our souls do not."

"Three with the Law of Attraction is that what you put out is what you get back."

"And four is that we can't stop change, like we can't stop growing old or our transition back to our souls."

"Excellent the law you might have forgotten is everything is here and now. Everything exists now, even what you feel might be considered a past life like Norma Jean."

"You know about her?"

"Your higher self-let you peek into that fractal to see the rabbit trail you were going down again. I don't know if you recall that your insistence that extraterrestrials exist in a time when the planet wasn't ready got you into hot water in that reality."

I feel like she is why I've always known that extraterrestrials exist, and they have been part of earth for far longer than I can imagine.

"That's called Karma or the last universal law that states what you put out is what you get back. You put out hate, you get hate back. You put out nonjudgement then you get nonjudgement back."

We're back to the law of attraction. It gets around.

"You got it. So anything else you need assistance with?"

"I'm tired tonight, but can you come back tomorrow night? I'd love to talk more about the universe. Say Hi to my grandma Mary and all in the spirit realm."

"I'll tell you what, we'll be back for twelve nights in a row. We'll call it a baker's dozen. Sleep well Mona Lisa. Sleep well. You never know who might stop by for a nightly visit."

"Thank you, Grandfather. Can I call you grandfather?"

"I've been waiting for sixty years for you to ask. Now I have had a dream come true, let's see if I can't do the same for you. Good night."

Download  2
MOTHER MARY: WE ARE SOURCE
June 6

Dearest Grandfather,

"Hello! I'm back!"

"Yes, my child so we come in much love with much love for you. We are here with a council to answer any questions you might have for us today."

"Really? I mean I might need a few minutes, hours, or days to get my head wrapped around that. I'm here as a vessel of love to deliver any messages you might want to deliver to others at this time."

"Thank you. I'll let Mother Mary speak first."

"Hello Mona Lisa. Greetings. We come with love. There are many messages we would like to deliver but there is one for you. Our messages we have spoken and will continue to speak to all that are ready to hear us. We see you struggle with your self-worth. Why my child? You are made of the same star dust, the same God Source as we are. Understanding your value cannot be measured in human words. As Bashar and others have taught, you are part of the whole and the whole is part of you. Without you, God is not complete."

"Funny, well kind-of, I started this journey wanting to achieve this and that. Like always striving for the next mountain to climb and now I see the mountain to climb is the one inside of me."

"Very well said, very well indeed. Do you love without measure? Do you strive to live in the

moment? These are quite real human challenges for most. Many will put conditions on love. Is it love if it's conditional? Living in the now for the now and not the past or the future can also deprive one of joy. This is not to say that one should not consider the future consequences or forget lessons from the past, but one should not dwell on them. Decide the best plan of action because of either the past lesson or future desires and go forward living in the present. One may begin with why am I choosing that? Is it a decision that is best for you? Let's say one wants a new house... Why? Is it to be more creative? Could you find ways to be just as creative in the space you reside presently? Maybe you want a new job, one that pays more, but you're happy where you are at. Can you ask for a raise? Figure out a way to live within your means? Expansion is a wonderful thing and maybe it's best, and time for you to move on. Asking oneself 'why' when you desire something on the earth plane will help you decide if it's a good decision.

"I'm beginning to see why many say the awakening as spiritual human beings with a human body is a process."

"Yes, very well said. When you reach one plateau are you ready for the next?"

"The more I know the more I realize the less I know. How high can we go?"

"Recall the day of 911 and you felt your heart surrounded and full of love? You were sad for all the deaths and destruction, but you did not let it take away your light. When you can do that on a consistent basis then you know you've mastered the earth plane and sit in the fifth dimension."

"Sometimes I have felt guilty for having love in my heart that day. It was a day that spirit had filled me up with love like I had being hugged from spirit."

"You were being held by your inner being and you felt it. Was there anything you could have done at all to stop the deaths on 911? Would one ounce of guilt help support that day in any way? Guilt is not love. Guilt does not benefit anyone involved. It keeps the light from shining as bright as it possibly can. We are not saying to look at feelings like grief or guilt when they come up. It is wise to look at them and understand why you are feeling that emotion. Recall when you feel grief or guilt you are not looking at it like your inner being. "

"Today I choose to live in the now."

"Much love to you. Until our paths cross again."

"My own heart is full. Thank you, thank you all for your wisdom. I see that I have much to work on. My friends are right. I need to work on me, now, and now me."

"You are so very welcome."

"I wish I could shout it out to the mountain top all your teachings, but I get this feeling that it has been done again and again."

"Be the light where you are, be the soul living in the now and understanding that you are love, you are spirit and let your cup overspill with joy. That is enough to be the example."

I wish everyone could see we are spirit beings in a body and our souls live for an eternity.

"That is correct, so why the rush? You be the best you that you can be. Be the light by being the love."

"So easy and yet challenging at the same time."

"No challenge, all easy. I would not necessarily use that word 'challenging' or it might come back to be difficult for you."

"Yes, we are the god's of our words."

"Well said. Be the peace to you."

"My love to you and the council."

"Ours to you."

"I am so blessed."

"You are, and I feel you are beginning to see the truth. That in every moment we all have abundance and glory around us."

"I wish that I knew years ago what I know now. I would have lived differently."

"Take that wish and turn it into now's reality. Continue to show peace within you and show the love of source within you."

"With all my heart I feel gratitude to you."

"Well done my child. Remember don't be so hard on yourself. You are in the toughest school in the universe. You are doing perfectly for you."

"Thank you."

With a smile and a wink, Mother Mary's energy and voice was gone.

I feel a tear roll down my face. Not of sorrow. No, these tears are for the overwhelming love that I feel bathed in from head to toe. Part of me knows that tomorrow, I will partially forget who I am. I will partially forget that I am that I am, that my great great grandfather 63 generations back is Yeshua, and my great great grandmother is Mother Mary 64 generations back! Oh, what blood runs through my veins! How did I not know this? Now, I do. What do I do with it? Maybe Grandfather will answer me tomorrow.

I am blessed. I am blessed beyond measure. I am, I am joy, I am love, I am abundance, I am one with source, I am sooo grateful. I am a spirit in a fading body that will turn to spirit one day and likely, most likely return to a human body. Why? I know I lived before I've seen me in a Native American girl child's body. I've seen me in a movie star's body. I came back, and keep coming back. One reason might be because there's adventure in learning. Another reason might be there is growth in learning. There is challenge in being human and most of all because expansion is change and change is expansion. Change is a constant in the Universe.

Download ❀ 3
THOUGHTS WITH GOD
June 7

What a day! What a day! So last night my inner being in a dream asked me to go down a dark tunnel in a mist of blackness, but before I could, the alarm went off.

As I went on my walk in the woods today, I saw myself with an alien being go down that tunnel we ended up in a sea of water becoming water like beings with scales on our extremities, enlarged webbed feet and hands, and very little hair.

We swam and swam. He showed me an underwater structure made of large squarish stones, mostly covered in seaweed and other underwater marine life. One thing that stuck out about the building was that I could tell where some of the edges of the stones were by how the marine life was growing on it. Thick or thin at the edges and or creases.

We swam along the stones until we came to the other side where the alien placed his webbed hand on the stone so that we could enter.

We entered into a small, square room with white lights around the ceiling. First, we shook off the water then as we left the room a blow dryer of sorts blowing on us as we walked down a short corridor to a large room. The room was busy with aliens at a bar visiting with one another.

I caught a tall Nordic looking one glancing at us, but they quickly turned away. My alien friend led me to a small pub table where we sat down at. He only communicated with me telepathically asking how I liked the place.

I told him I loved the wall of glass that looked out into the ocean. It looked black except when a fish would swim by. The next thing I knew is a small dish is placed in front of me. He encourages me to try it.

"Tastes like butter," I say.

"Fruit butter," he reassures me. He tells me it's time to go. I'm sad, as we just arrived, but the next thing I know it's time for my friend's meditation night.

I had no idea of her planned meditation for that evening. She took us remote viewing out to the Atlantic Ocean…to see what we can see in the ocean near a large underwater structure.

I've already been there! Chalk one up for being intuitive.

I ponder, "Great Grandfather Yeshua, how real was it all?"

I can hear my inner being asking, "Does it matter?"

I want to see, yes! Yes it matters, otherwise I'm crazy with my imagination.

I hear laughter.

"Remember your teachings… Where does the imagination come from?"

Source, our imagination comes from our inner being who is directly connected to ALL. Like Dr. Wayne Dyer says, the ego says, "your thoughts are very important. The Holy Spirit insists, "Only thoughts you think with God are real—nothing else matters."

Download ✸ 4
I AM THE DANCE
June 8.

Dearest Grandfather Yeshua are you here today?

> *"Always. Are you here today?"*

"I am." We laugh.

> *"Wait here,"* I hear a voice in my head speak.

I feel His presence leave. I still feel His love but it's not as overpowering as when He's in my mind's eye. Then I see the tall fish humanoid alien from yesterday.

"It's you."

> *"Who did you think it was going to be?"*

"Are you real?"

> *"I am."*

Do you really look like a fish being?

> *"For the moment. I am a 12th dimensional being.*
> *More like a geometric sphere of light."*

I look at the tall blue fish-man. I want to say, there is no such thing as a 12th dimensional being, but what do I know? "Can you look like who or whatever you desire?"

The tall blue figure nodded yes. I met the kind eyes and I feel my actual body fill with love energy like when I'm in the presence of my great grandfather or an angel. "What message do you have for me?"

> *"That you are loved. Do you have a question for*
> *me?"*

"What was that down the tunnel and swim in the ocean all about?

"Did not you ask for more intuitiveness?"

I nod yes. "How to raise my vibration."

"Love yourself more. One way is to forgive yourself. Tell yourself that you forgive yourself of all things great and small. Take a shower and pretend it's a shower of purple stream washing away yesterday's mistakes. Be one. Do you remember the girl child from a parallel lifeline?"

"That was, and is a part of me?"

"Yes, sending yourself love from one life to another because you are one, part of all. Love, breathe, and be happy. Do what makes your heart sing. Remember? Do you remember her poem to you?"

"Yes!"

"Can you repeat it for me here? I'd love to hear it. It was like music to one's ears on how to raise vibration."

I took a deep breath and recalled the American native ten-year-old child. I have only briefly met her, but I know each moment she has always been with me. She lives! She lives in me. I began to recite her poem:

I AM
I am one.
One is all.
All is one.

I am.
Exploring.

Downloads from One Consciousness

Becoming.
Learning.
Being.
Life in life.
Exciting.
Discovering the light in the dark.
Falling in the dark, swimming to the crack of light.
Basking in the light. Catching the dark, sticking my tongue at it,
laughing my way into the light.

I know I am light. Darkness is a guide to say go the other way.
Darkness is made by self.
Light by the One.
Go to the One.
Go to the One, go to the light…see the cracks in the darkness.

Peace, tranquility, home is there in knowing all is one, one is all.
Light is within.
Ask, discover, breathe… Just breathe.

Be.
Be you.
That is enough.
Your worth is immeasurable.
Source is not complete without you.

You are more loved and supported than you will ever know.
You are loved and supported as much as you allow.
You are loved.
You are loved.
You are loved unconditionally forever more.

Rest, breathe, for you shall always be.
It is best to be you.
Be you. Be yourself.

Find what makes your heart sing, and sing that tune. I guarantee
you that no one will and does sing that tune just like you. You are
you.
Be you and be complete.
Be complete by being you.
It's a song, it's a dance.
It's a play and you set the stage, set up the players, now you are
free to be you.

Free.
You have freedom to see the light.
You have freedom to see the dark.
Pick the light with song and dance.
You ARE.
You are complete.
Perfect in every unperfect way.
That's the glory in it all.
No imperfections that are not perfect, you are being you.
Be you.
Be you.

Dance to the song you hear in your heart.
Let the stars fall.
Let life sing.
Joy within brings endless melodies.
Face the mountains; no fear.
Climb any and every way you can as time and distance does not
matter.
Be bold. Be alive.
When sadness comes, be okay.
Embrace the grief and let it go like leaves that turn brown on an
autumn tree.
Remember after the snow comes spring. Let sadness flow away
from you like the melting snow from the mountain top.

All is good.
You are good; don't forget.

So free to see all the good and all the bad. Free to choose either.
Free to choose either.
When you sit at the bottom with your woes remember you are
free to choose either
Light within, God within says choose life…live, love, and laugh.
That is, it.
That is the secret to life. Eat smart, breathe in the fresh air as
you love your life, and above all make room for laughter.
Laughter is medicine for the soul.
Like water is energy for the body, breath for the spirit.
Do not rush for there is no end.

Let me give you this, you are eternal and will not complete it all
in this one trip!
Your days, you have picked before you came.
So go ahead and embrace your life. Live. Live. Live.
Your time to turn into a butterfly is not yet at hand.
Be happy.
Dance to your own tune.
Let the rest go.
Be you. Be you. Be the imperfect, perfect you.
What the rest say is inconsequential. What others think is none
of your business.
Your business is you. YOU.
You for the rest of eternity.
Only you to heal, learn, and know your soul.
Understand it all begins and ends with you.

You are the one.
One is all.
Undertake no-one else's responsibilities, jobs, roles.
Freedom in that gift.
The greatest gift is life.
You chose now. Now can be hard if you define it so…
Define it easy, accept it easily. It's easy to breathe and be.
It's natural to be you.
If it's hard, is it you?

Let the hardness go. Let the old definitions go.
Life is eternal.
Enjoy the ride.
You're here on this little blue spinning ball for a blink of an eye.
The least you can do is to enjoy.
Enjoy the climb, the fall, the dirt in your shoes!
Why not?
If it weighs you down, then it's not your path.
Let it go.

So many paths to choose, choose any, pick, dance, and pick
again.
Enjoy the now.
Be one with trees, the bees, and me.
I am you.
You are me.
I am.
I am.
I am
Home.

**"Beautiful, so beautifully said. The world needs
to hear that you know, so they too can raise their
vibrations. If you ever forget reread that poem."**

What do I say, "An alien told me to shout this poem?"

"Am I alien to you?"

"Not at all."

"It's your dance."

"Thank you." In my mind's eye I see the water entity vanish. I
wonder if he was real. My heart beating in my chest when I looked
into his eyes, tells me he was very real. All I felt was kindness,
goodness, and love.

Downloads from One Consciousness

The more I learn, the less I know. I know that I feel love from head to toe. I look up and say thanks. I feel tears in my eyes. I swallow and I'm full of humbleness to be so filled with love.

"Learning is a process," I hear that inner voice say.

I grin as I think about tomorrow. I wonder if Grandfather's consciousness will stay, or introduce me to yet another spirit.

Download ✸ 5
HOW TO LIVE A WONDERFUL LIFE
June 9

"Hello Grandfather Yeshua! How is spirit life?"

"Wonderful. How is spirit life with your feet on the ground as they say?"

"Wonderful, because I get to talk to you and so many wonderful spirit beings. Thank you, thank you all."

"Do you have a question?"

"Were you killed on the cross?"

"You know the answer to that. What is your real question?"

"How will anyone ever believe me?"

"Who cares? That's doubt talking, so take it and put in the trash with a very tight lid. Rest in knowing that I Am that I Am."

"I am that I am. I do have ears that hears your consciousness and a heart that feels your love."

"What are your gifts my granddaughter?"

"Love, inspiration, writer, swimmer, compassion, and teacher."

"Do you follow your passion?"

"Sometimes."

"Why only sometimes?"

"I go to work from seven to four, five days a week. Clean on the weekends. I must do what I must do."

"How does it make you feel?"

"Worthless."

*"No-one can make you feel worthless unless you
let them."*

"I'm working it. I know that I'm your granddaughter. I know that I might be off my soul path. Still, I get up and do the best I know…not the best I wish, want, or desire."

*"You know you deserve to be happy every day.
One does that by listening to God, Source inside
of them. You can do that no matter where you
are. That was part of my own teaching that God
lives within find that source of energy and let it
burn bright let all else go.*

"Yes, I can. I can say it is easy and the day will be easy. I say I'm going to have a wonderful day and ten out of ten days it is, but then I forget and every bone hurts to get up. Down that winding path I go."

*"One does not see what they are not ready to
see."*

"I'm ready. Maybe it's that Ego piece that ties me to the physical plane."

*"Give it a bone and slowly the physical you will
see that your spiritual side knows what, where it's
leading you."*

"I like that. I like that a lot. What bone may I feed the ego?"

*"Tell it that you are listening to it and
compromise, negotiate a win, win scenario for
the physical and spiritual side of you.*

"One compromise I came up with is when I can bring in 10% of my now income on my joy, passion then I'll quit my work. Secondly,

I'll work one more year so that I can earn 25% of my income in an early retirement."

"You are on a solid path. Why are you so hard on yourself?"

"Because I did not give up my physical job for a life following my passion like you."

"Don't be in such a hurry, there's always the next time and the next time after that. One has eternity you know. What goals do you have for yourself this year?"

"To learn all I can spiritually about souls, spirit, aliens, love, and the God, Source within us."

"One may spend a lifetime on one of those topics."

"Yeah, I've always kind of done overboard."

"How has that worked out for you?"

We laugh and the candle blows out. Spirit has ascended back into the realm where I'm finding it easier and easier to ascend. I like it there. "There" is filled with love from head to toe. I can do anything, maybe I'm only a wisp of energy, but I feel like me.

"Don't be in a hurry," I feel a voice in the wind.

"I take it at 60 I still have a lot of learning to do." I laugh and go outside for a long walk in the woods. Me and my pups walk among the tall trees, smell the pines, and see a red-tailed hawk soar above. As we meander down the road there is a deer in a meadow far away. When we finally get to the small lake, we see a family of geese swimming across the middle. I stop to give thanks to Gaia. Directly before we make it back home a rabbit scurries off in the tall weeds. This is heaven. Grandpa is right, I'm in no hurry to leave this place. I'd miss the bunnies.

Download  6
SYNCHRONICITIES!
June 10

Today's letter came in the form of a request. As I awoke, I heard a voice say for today's letter write the Synchronicity events of last week. That's the letter.

This will be easy for me to write, as that is what comes easy for me. Telling, the stories verbally… well I haven't got that part down YET. I will, I can, I am that I am. I am a storyteller too!

Here are the Synchronicities in my life from last week:

I woke up and listened to a podcast about angels. A lady who channels angels said if you have a question or request for them, ask. They love to show you they are real.

"Archangel Michael," I asked. "Am I on the right path? Show me. I desire to be a medium. If it's in the cards that I should be, show me. I'm here. I'm listening." I said a prayer close to that as I did my Saturday morning walk in our local woods.

Within an hour, I was channeling a lady's airedale (farming/hunting dog). The lady mentioned to me how much she was missing her dog that recently died. "I said something like, "she isn't gone," and closed my eyes, I heard quite plainly. "I love you Mommie, I love you Mommie." The lady nearly cried when I relayed the message. She also wants you to know. "She'll wait for you and is always near."

Inside I was nearly crying with joy! Angels work fast! Thank you Archangel Michael. Much love and gratitude toward you!

The next thing I know it's 5:55 on my clock Monday morning. I normally wake up at 4:50 and try to have a cup of coffee and be dressed by 5:45 to do a walk with the dogs before work. Ten minutes late, but it's the last week before a much-needed break from work. Angelically 555 means a change is in the works.

That day a co-worker asks me a very strong question that I've heard others ask, but when she asked me directly it touched me deep. We both shared that morning we knew of two separate young men at 19 and 20 who had just committed suicide. She asked when Jesus is coming back. He needs to do it now. I bite my tongue. Doesn't she know he *is* back? He's back to anyone who has an open heart and is willing to learn that he is there for them. He will talk to you, and I do mean talk. He will show himself to you. He comes to me as a warm golden glow. I will place a piece of artwork below, which is how I see him, surrounded in a golden light. I am not alone. So many channelers hear from him as well. Grandpa's message is that of love, love, nonjudgement, and more love.

So I came home that day and wrote the very first letter to Him, and now you see it too. That was the beginning of synchronicities in the week...

I think higher vibration realms wanted to send a strong message, a message of love, a message of truth beyond the vail if I dare to open my eyes to see.

Grandpa said have sweet dreams. That night I saw my spirit guide asking me if I wanted to go down a dark tunnel as we were out in the middle of space. As I was about to say yes, the alarm went off!

I wondered what it was about all day. On my walk I got the

download I wrote about above. The one with the alien taking me for a swim. Then Courtney's meditation out to the Atlantic Ocean to see what was there. Can you imagine how I felt? I had just been there! Talk about synchronicities lined up. Spirit says the more on the path you are, the more synchronicities rain upon your path. I see my path! Today I dance for my heart is full, my path is clear. Angels, Yeshua, Mother Mary, Archangel Michael, and all other spirit beings and aliens, I love you all so much for showing me my path. Love and gratitude, love and appreciation. You got this 60 year old crying with good news that it's not too late to wake up and follow your highest good. It's never too late!

Yeshua in my visions is in a golden glow.

Download ✸ 7
TEACHINGS OF YESHUA
June 11

"Hello Great Grandfather Yeshua!"

"Hello Mona Lisa. I like my name today."

"Yes, it took me several days, but I like it too. It feels right. How are you?"

Laughing. "I'm spirit. Things are beautiful now, now, and now." Whispering he continued, "That means yesterday, today, and tomorrow."

I laughed. "They say you can't have new experiences on the other side, but since you are communicating with me. Isn't this new, at least for us?

"You have a way of cutting to the chase. An ascended soul can't have new experiences in the sense they can't experience grief, break a leg, or eat a meal. They might smell the flowers or a good meal through you. They can and will support you, so these are a few things souls can do. I'm sure that is clear as mud."

"Did you have the sayings like 'cutting to the chase' and 'clear as mud' when you on the ground?"

"No, but I know your expressions."

"So you use symbolism so that I may create a picture and thus better remember your teachings."

"Exactly."

"Beautiful. Do you know the alien named Bashar?"

"One consciousness."

"He talks of you and other great master teachers. Says they were all trying to teach that love, source, is inside each of us and if we listen to God, the Source, Our inner being, Our Soul inside of us then we will become alchemist of life. My heart tells me that is what you were teaching."

"That is what I teach."

Laughing. "Why can I hear, but not see?"

"I think you can hear and see just fine. Letting go is like taking a big breath and saying I am Love.

All as in God that will give me what I need when I need it and the rest let go, let go, let go."

Practice it. Pretend someone says cruel things about you. How will you handle it?"

"I am. I am that I am. I am love. What they say is not a reflection of me, but of them. I let what they say go. I let it go and concentrate on the sun, the birds in the air, my dogs, family, dive into a meditation, or anything else that gets me back to center. Easy for me to say, and my words have power so now it will be easy for me to do."

Laughing. "I see you growing, glowing right before my eyes."

Laughing. "I wish you, the council, archangels and all the spirit world love and appreciation. Thanks for your guidance and love.

"You're so welcome. Why do I see tears?"

"I think I know how you felt as they sentenced you. Alone and wondering if they would believe you if you spoke, so you didn't because it was all said already."

*"Remember my teachings and the all the days
that I was lined up with the God within."*

"Okay. I remember that you taught do not judge least you be judged."

"Yes, I did. What rings truth for you in that?"

*Nonjudgement is the way to live. To see life
through source we know instinctively that the
beggar and the king are seen on equal terms. If
one thinks differently or has a different opinion
than you, that's okay. Don't judge it. Maybe it's
not your truth, but try to understand that one's
truth is not necessarily, nor does it ever have to be
your truth. If it rings true in your heart then you
know it is true for you. "Most get it at a simple
level, it's when they feel fear or threatened then
it's out the window."*

Laughing. "Yes, especially now. I feel, I sense it turning more positive. My circle believes in nonjudgement. I have these friends that I met and each and every one I know you'll be so proud of me that I have such loving and caring friends. I think you've met one, Staci?"

*"Yes, I've met laughing Staci. That is a glorious
group of friends."*

"I am so loved."

"Yes, you are."

"Worthy of your radiant aura." Yeshua winks at
me and is gone.

I feel tears run down my face and I know today's lesson will be with me for quite some time. I'm going for my walk to feel my grandfather in the wind, in the trees, in the rocks, inside of me, and know when I do I'm feeling God, I'm feeling me. I know that when I look at the trees that it will be God looking at the trees expanding by each of my breaths. When I see the critters on my walk, I will know that the same Source lives within them, expanding, living, and being. As I feel the cool late evening wind on my face, Yeshua will feel it too as He is God, God is me, and we are one. I am no less than the most exalted nor am I any more than the trees and the animals as we are part of Source, part of God, each a puzzle piece that makes the One whole.

Today is my new beginning and I don't think I'll look at the world in 3D again. Tears run down my face not for sadness, but to wash way the old view. To welcome the new view. I am One, One is me, All are One. One is the All. How many times have I heard that, but today I feel it.

Thank you All for caring so much about this One to lift her up to be All in her oneness.

Download ✪ 8
MARILYN MONROE'S DEATH
June 12

"Dear Great Grandfather Yeshua and all benevolent beings of the light!"

"Hello! I come with much appreciation and love. What would you have to write about today?

"Explain the dream," I heard my inner being tell me.

"When I woke up I saw in my mind's eye a crystal glass ceiling breaking over my head. Don't worry, I got up and moved before the shards fell onto to me as they fell on the bed."

"I thought about it all day. I wondered, like the last dream, what it meant. I did have a clue from our previous conversations, but I knew it had to be something deep, something that once I shared with the world there was no going back."

"Then Dr. Steven Greer gave a live presentation on extraterrestrials. He was listing dirty deeds done by a secret government within the United States. He listed and showed a picture of Marilyn Monroe's death warrant two days before she died due to the fact she knew that aliens were real, that Roswell was real from her connection with Robert Kennedy. My heart went ballistic, it seems that my oversoul has a piece of her soul born Norma Jean Baker. Jeanie, as I call her, for that is the nickname she told me when I asked for a name.

I never knew I had any connection to Marilyn at all. I mean why should I? I was born with a strong belief that aliens are real and they are why we are our humanness today. I've just known. Is it an innate knowing, like duh?

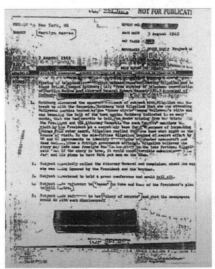

Marilyn Monroe Death Warrant (Greer 2023)

Anyway, back to Jeanie, way, way before I learned about the details of Jeanie's death, I began checking out my past lives. I saw me during the Atlantis times, then as a native girl, and then someone from the 50's. I described them to my hubby. He says you're describing Marilyn Monroe. I of course in all rationality said not likely.

So being the strong spirit that I am, I asked my inner being who she was, and I got a very vivid picture of Jeanie in my vision. There was no denying the blonde bombshell, it was Marilyn Monroe. Shortly after, while meditating, I asked why she has come to me now. I pop out of my body (astral projecting) and go to the shreds of light and there I am… I land in 1962. I'm answering the door of a southwestern type of home with a green door. I recognize the black official looking car as a government type, but I don't look like me, I am Marilyn. Two men in black suits are at the door. One asks to use the restroom. I nodded okay and let him in. The other tells me that I'd better be quiet regarding the information I have threatened to come out with regarding aliens or it will not go well for me. He asked me if I understood. The other returns and I tell them both, "It's time to leave."

I'm scared down to my toes. I go to the kitchen. There's a bottle with a beautiful new opener next to it. I take a drink, then another as I feel like getting drunk. I had no idea the alcohol was laced with drugs.

I get sick to my stomach and take off my dress as I feel myself wanting to up-heave, I pass out cold by the toilet and that's the last thing I remember before I pop out of my body. I don't know how I made it back to bed. Maybe I wasn't dead yet and tried to go call for help. I don't remember at this point. That is not important. What is important is that I understand that I am a spirit and spirit will guide me to my highest good.

Knowing what I just learned several months ago, I ran to a past life regressionist where the first time Jeanie did not pop up. It was my Native American self, young girl of ten who you already met. I had asked for a message for my highest good and all those who might hear it, the answer came from the young girl, it wasn't Jeanie.

I asked my inner being why did Jeanie come to me now at 60? What I first received was the alien connections, but since that time it's also been an outlook on life. All Jeanie wanted was love of a good man and a family. Her dreams have come true this time around. Her and my great challenges in our lives has been the feeling of self-worth. I have a piece of art on my wall that says, "Worthiness is truth." I believe, but my soul will rise when I know it. At times I know it, then well… I sink back down to earth. Which is ironic since mother earth has so much worthiness in her, in trees, in flowers. Yes, I want to know I'm as worthy as the plants of the earth! Did you know plant vibrations are higher than most humans? Truth!

Before I write, I ask spirit and Yeshua to give me the message they want to give, they want me to write and that above is what flowed. I am abundantly loved as we all are. Will you let yourself be loved today?

Download ✹ 9
Jeanie Out of the Bottle
June 13

Dearest Great Grandfather Yeshua, Council, Aliens, Angels and Spirits on the Other side:

Does anyone have a message today that would like to convey?

"I do. It's me, Jeanie. Hello Mona Lisa. I'm speaking to you from our oversoul. How are you? My desire was not to send you down a rabbit hole. My desire was to let you know that we have commonalities. Your highest wish is to be abundant in love, family, friendship, and in knowing that the Universe has your back. I promise you it does.

"Say after me, "I am happy right now, I am happy right now, I am happy right now. That's one of the greatest secrets from us on this side to you. All we have is now, and now, and now. No matter what the rain, hardship, tell yourself I am happy and rest in the knowing of it. Sit back and watch the magic."

"You got this woman. You are alive. You are alive. Your soul which does contain a small piece of me is always with you. You are part of the Great Knowing, God, Source, whatever you want to call the Infinite. WE are one. I am proud that you are part of the great time on earth. I mean, seriously after my drugs and alcohol fight do you think I would have lived to be ninety-two? Love, love, love, love, and love."

*"I feel it in you that you got this. I'm leaving now.
I will always be with you. You need to be you.
Not me. Be YOU and I will shine. I love you; I
love you, I love you. PS Can you send Elton John
that little poem you wrote, I think he'd get a kick
out of it.
Best of luck, Jeanie."*

I see Jeanie blow me a kiss only like she could have done. The door in my mind's eye closes. I feel like weeping, but as I write the words, I feel an undeniable hug from the other side. It says you are loved. This is not a time to cry, but to celebrate after all I am happy right now, I am happy right now.

Here you go knowing this is especially for Elton John:

I am

I am a long last.

I am a long last somebody.

Yet to ALL: I am a candle in the wind.

I am not blown away

Not blown out

I am

I am alive

I am alive living a dream under our night stars.

I am as happy as happy ever after gets.

I am

I am Mona Lisa

I am Norma Jean

Downloads from One Consciousness

I am Marilyn Monroe

I am spirit.

I am

I am letting you know.

The stars I dance under, light my way eternally.

I am not a blown-out candle in the wind.

My candle burns an eternal flame.

I am sixty this timeline.

I am; I am forever

I am free this time around to be me

To watch the tulips grow and chase rainbows

I am

I am forever grateful for your song about me as Norma Jean

Now I'm Mona Lisa

My gift to you is we all are eternal.

Now we've only met through words.

I am not Marilyn Monroe, that was an act I embraced.

I am Mona Lisa

With love,

From Norma Jean (aka) Mona Lisa Coburn
Reborn in August of 1962 (Three weeks after Jeanie's death)
5'5-1/2 inches just like Jeanie.
Special Education Teacher, Channeler, with 3 adult children, and a
hubby of 40 years.

Download ✸ 10
CHAKRAS AND RAINBOWS
June 14

Dearest Great Grandfather Yeshua and all spiritual beings,

"I send you the greatest love and appreciation for all the words, you have filled my soul. Thank you for them. Thank you for all the beautiful downloads thus far. I am overflowed with joy and happiness. Thank you."

I hear a whisper to write about the rainbow.

The rainbow was in our sky two days ago after a brief thunderstorm. Like a child, I went hurrying chasing it to see if I could catch a better picture of it.

As I chased it I thought wow is that what I have been doing my entire existence chasing rainbows? Talk about hitting home, remember I'm sixty years old. Chasing rainbows sounds fun, doesn't it? But when you always just think the grass is greener over there, the rainbow somehow more fulfilling over there, over there lies tranquility then you miss the now. Now is all we have and now and now. You get the picture.

There's a rainbow inside of you just waiting to burst forth. Like the rainbow, we are said to have certain areas within that illuminate all the colors of the rainbow and if we are wise enough to illuminate them we reflect love, a reflection of the one true happiness. We each have a source of eternal rainbows right inside of us. No need to go out there.

Most refer to the rainbow chakras inside of us starting at our root (tailbone) reflected by red, second slightly higher up is the orange chakra, third yellow chakra at our navel area, 4th is our heart chakra reflected green, 5th is the throat chakra reflected light blue, 6th

is third eye reflected indigo (deep purplish blue), 7th chakra is
reflected violet. There are more chakras like the spiritual ones above
the crown are reflected white, clear crystals. Some even talk about
one at our knees and ankles, but you get the idea. The idea of chakras
is as old as our humanity and stems from our galactic origins.

When I first heard about them, I thought, "What? What do you
say? Chakra what?" Now I feel them and can work with them by
slowing down and feeling my responses to what I say, what I do, or
my response to others or the environment around me. It's like the
more I tune into my inner being, the more I understand we are truly
spiriting down here on the earth plane for the fun of it, for the
adventure of it. For the most part all we can do is enjoy the ride. The
ride, the journey. It's about discovering the rainbow inside of us and
not chasing the rainbows outside of us unless it's what our greatest
excitement is at that moment, then go for it!

Download ✦ 11
YESHUA: EACH ONE IS I AM
June 15

Dearest Grandfather Yeshua and all,

"Today I send you more love than ever, but I do come with a heavy heart. Grandpa you said 13 days of visits, so it's getting close with eleven of them so far."

> *"No need for a heavy heart. When your heart is heavy, what does that tell you?"*

"That I'm not looking at it from Source's perspective."

> *"You seem to have the knowledge, but can you walk the talk? Can you rest knowing that the universe has your back? Can you pull out that rainbow and let your light shine? I know you can."*

> *"Now my dear grandchild write and know every time you do we all are here with Source, your inner being to guide you to write words on the page to make the brightest of rainbows. We are the rainbow.*
> *You are the rainbow."*

> *"If we had one more thing to tell the Universe it would be to love each one and for each and every one to love each other. I was trying to tell people back in my day that God, Source lives within. You knew that and lost it. Why do you think that was?"*

"I was living and breathing 3rd density. Now, I know without a shadow of doubt that I will never go back."

"Be you, live in love and happiness and watch the
Universe unfold your path before your feet. You
got this."

"You sound like my mother, my friends, and all those who get me."

"We are abundant!"

"We are very abundant."

"Live in love and happiness and goodness shall
rain upon you all the days of your life!"

"Thank you, great grandfather, with love and appreciation, so much love and appreciation!"

"The honor is ours. Now go tell the world that our wish is
for each and every one to discover God within and understand
we are all One Consciousness. Each one is I am. You wanted
your higher path? You wanted to break the glass ceiling, let the
shards fall and know this child, you are more loved and
supported than you shall ever know!"

"Let them see the blood line and know that you
are of the Magdalene bloodline. Rest in peace,
joy, and happiness. We celebrate who you are. I
know who you are...and I am proud. I love you.
Do you not think there was a reason why we
waited until 60 to impart these messages to you?"

"I know, I know, I know as I feel it down to my very being, my heart, my soul, my spirit."

"We are all One. One is the All. I am that I am. I am the great granddaughter of Yeshua, Jesus Christ, and I promise on my grave these words are the truth as I see it, as I know it to be."

"Love to you all. May those with ears hear these words, heed them. With those who have sight to read them, heed them. With those who have heart to sense them rest in the peace and joy that Yeshua is not dead. He is alive and will talk to you just as he talks to me. HE is Source. You are Source. We are One."

Amen.

Amen.

Amen.

Now go forth and be happy resting in knowing that you are eternal, joy comes lighting the rainbow within, and rest in joy. If the council had one more message it would be this: Be happy now, and now, and now, and now, for you are living in Heaven on Earth. Heaven is not separate from us, but here with us. Let your light shine no matter where you go, understand that is enough. That is what is needed at this time on Earth.

Amen.

Amen.

Amen

Mona Lisa Carr Coburn, Great Granddaughter of Yeshua, Jesus Christ and Mary Magdaline.

Download ❀ 12:
The Journey IS the Destination
June 16

I woke up this morning and heard a voice say, "continue the downloads."

Here I am at 7:54 at the word processor after a beautiful walk with the dogs and time with ALL.

"Spirits, Holy Spirit, God, Source, Yeshua, and ALL Beings part of all who would like to come through this morning? What message do you have for us living in the 3D plane? Is there anything that hasn't already been said?"

"We could write volumes and volumes that has not been brought to the light. Do you see your own flashlight? Do you remember where you shine is not necessarily where others shine their light. All lights are welcome and essential. WE are happy to assist in you this way. Let us fill your heart and let love fill the page."

"I feel like I'm speaking to the council. Is that correct?"

"It is."

"What questions do you have for us today?"

"I'm torn between two paths. One is financial security and the other is my passion. When I was in direct conversation with my Grandfather it was like, Duh which path to pick. I even have a plan of how and when to get off the path I'm on. Still, I've heard about switching realities. Can I switch my reality just like that and be in the one that has a million dollars in the bank?"

"Do you believe that all things are possible?"

"I do. I know that all things are possible. I mean, I'm talking to you all and feel that speaking with you is far more abundant than any paper money. I've learned if what you desire is not becoming real then one must have some underlying belief that is keeping you from that reality."

"That is correct. Can we ask you what is your hurry? Remember it's all about the journey. The journey is the destination."

"I really don't want to go back to work in a few weeks, because it no longer represents my highest joy. For me it represents money and exhaustion. I like having this newfound energy. I was up by six and by six thirty was happily walking my puppies."

"Yes, you will find energy springs like a well that can't be emptied when you are in the zone of your passion. It's like time flies when you are working on what you love, what you were called to do."

"I've tried many times to come out of the writing closet, but so far the doors keep shutting.

"The Universe wasn't ready to hear your words. Do you think they are ready now?

"Yes, I know that they are ready. My concern now is how to get it out there."

"Why is that your concern? I thought you enjoyed writing. Let getting it out there be ours."

"Remember when Karen Carpenter came to you?"

"Like it was a moment ago!"

"That's a great story. Maybe it's time you shared it, so you can remember the lesson and share it at the same time."

The story goes like this. about exactly a year ago I was wondering if I should go back to work for another year or not. I was meditating on it and praying about it. The topic of concerts came up and I thought to myself a regret of mine is not going to one of Karen Carpenter's concerts. I would love to go to a Karen Carpenter concert. The next morning after meditation, I heard a woman's voice I didn't recognize say, "Bless the Beasts and the Children."

I wondered what that meant. Later that day my hubby and I were driving to lunch. I asked him if he remembered the song called "God Bless the Beast and the Children?"

He said he vaguely remembered it. He pulled it up on his phone and played it on the car audio system. It wasn't "God Bless"…only "Bless the Beasts and the Children." And the voice coming out of the speakers was Karen!!!

We then listened to Karen Carpenter sing it again and again as if she was playing us a personal concert. I know in my heart; I know it to be truth that was Karen Carpenter telling me to play that song and answering a prayer that I needed to teach again for another year. Thank you, Karen! Since then, in my own way, I have channeled Karen. I feel her heart fill mine with love especially when I'm singing her songs. This is nothing new. All people do when they sing songs. I don't know how to sing on key, and I often wonder if it makes her laugh and laugh and laugh and laugh.

I am so filled with love from my head to my toes with appreciation for the council, for Karen Carpenter, and for all those who led and guided me. My spirit guides are vast, and I am abundant in love, friends, spirit, and the list is endless. Thank you, thank you, thank you. May love fill you up as it is filling me up. May you see

Heaven on Earth and understand that it is here for you and me and all those who truly see the truth.

I feel the candle blow out. Spirit has ascended, but I feel their love and I'm grinning with a stupid smile for I am loved.

Download ❀ 13
Exit Points
June 18

Dearest Great Grandfather Yeshua, Spirit and Spirit Guides,

"I have a question for you today. When will my mediumship abilities come more fully online?"

"When I always remember to get in the correct mindset by setting forward my intentions, clearing the space, and asking for messages from loved ones near for the highest good. Is that it?

> *"Meditation wouldn't hurt either. Having one that asks or is asking doesn't hurt either. Maybe ask one if they want a message. That's pretty much it."*

> *One's vibration needs to synchronize knowing they are loved, are from love, and forgiveness of self and others of past regression doesn't hurt. Maybe practicing theses in your daily routine would be helpful as well.*

> *Lighting your candle and asking spirits like guides to come in and assist you could be most helpful as well. Sitting, mediation, then asking for spirit guides to assist you before you actually go out and practice could be most helpful. Being at peace with oneself and others is very important. If one is off kilter then it's more difficult if not impossible to perceive messages from the other side.*

***Do you wish to communicate with someone at
this time?***

I wish spirit to bring forth one that needs to come through for
the highest good of them and me or my hubby who is in the room.

**"Hello, Mona Lisa." I hear the voice of Rob who
passed away during COVID lockdowns.
"How are you?"**

"I'm great. How's Heaven?"

**"Great. Tell Charlie that I appreciate that he
came to visit me."**

"I certainly will! Seriously, would you like me to give your
children a message or two?"

"Would you do that? Tell them that I'm always with them. Tell
them that I love them. We're here, their mother and I. We're in no
hurry as they keep us busy even on this side!"

"Can you tell me something that they would know it's a message
from you?"

"Tell them we were at exit points."

But doesn't one plan their return date?

**"Yes. The cancer was at a predestined natural
exit point. Tell my oldest she is doing fine. My
daughter, thanks too for the granddaughter. Our
son, he's stronger than he knows. And our
youngest that we are with her.**

**If they are still enough and listen, they will learn
to feel us. Tell them to try it. We send our love to
each of them!**

The candle is blown out. Spirit ascended back to Heaven.

Download ✖ 14
GIVE OF THE HEART TO GIVE SERVICE
June 19

Exciting day yesterday, selling *Universal Toolbox* at a local flea market. I believe my spirit was in an alien craft last night, as when I awoke, I was looking towards a large trapezoid window in a spaceship. I saw an alien being in the shadows and the ship was dark compared to the outside of the window which a brilliant light was emanating.

Synchronicity is coming hard and fast, in everything, everywhere. I am on the right path. I asked my inner being what I can do today to make the biggest difference for myself and others. All I heard was one word: "Write."

Writing is like the sweetest of sweetest music to my ears. I write and I am complete. The words and I are ONE. If you could only see the tears in my eyes as I write this…a single tear of bliss, joy rolls down my cheek. I momentarily stop as my eyes blur. God what do you want to say today? Let me move out of the way….just write, write through me and then I'll be WHOLE. We will be ALL in the Oneness.

> *"My Dearest Mona Lisa do not be fearful to be yourself more and more completely. Follow the softest of whispers of your soul. You are raising your vibration by being you, by forgiving yourself, and in the knowing of your soul that you are one with all and all with the One."*

Like the mist over the pond this morning, you let the love of Source flow over your human body and become a vessel of light, a vessel of higher vibrations. You are well on your way. You ask

what you can do to serve me today. I ask you
what you can do to serve yourself.
WRITE.

In writing you'll find higher vibrations, you'll find
love, you'll find yourself and you fulfill your
soul's purpose. Like Mozart was born to light the
world with his music, you were born to light the
world with your words. Feel its love on the page.
It feels like a warm bath, a hug from your
Bernese Mountain Dog, a drink of the finest
wine, a dance with Charlie to Karen Carpenter's
music, the smell of your mother's sugar cookies,
the morning sunrise, the evening sunset, the
swim when the water is not too cool nor too
warm, a walk in the woods among the tall pines
with needles underfoot and crisp morning air.
You get the picture. Any more questions today?

"I'm so humbled and filled with love. Thank you, thank you and words on a page don't seem like enough."

"They are enough as when you write from the
heart, you give of the heart in services and that
my young child is the meaning of life. Did you
not think those lessons we gave you in your
Dream Navigator novels, in your Universal
Toolbox books were not for you as well?"

"Write"

"We'll be there with you in spirit and in love with
every word as long as you continue to write with
love, for love, and the betterment of all."

Download ✥ 15
LIGHT WORKER
June 20

Dearest I Am, Source, God, Great Grandfather Yeshua, and ALL Spirit and Beings:

"To the top of the morning to you! To the top of the morning to you! Saying those words brings me joy, but today, this morning I am spilling tears as it is what I said most mornings to Hope. She is with you. How are you today Hope? I saw you walk in spirit form across the room the other day. Thank you! I felt so much love!"

"Hope, do you have anything you'd like to tell me today? I see you give me that great big doggy grin in my mind's eye.

I hear you say, *'I love you and I'm here. No need for tears. You gave me a grand life full of walks, adventures, and love. Thank you.'*

"I miss you today. I miss your beingness."

"Don't cry mommy. I love you."

I stop and cry. It seems whether dog or human, when we lose the ones we love the most there always seems to be room for tears. May the creator in me see that grief is part of love and although creation does not look at transition as death, may it understand that us here miss the physical form once the spirit passes into the light.

I am blessed to talk to spirit the way I can. I am blessed to talk to other dimensional beings the way I can. I am blessed in that I know that I am spirit living in this 3-D world for just a short while. I understand the best we can do is to enjoy it for 100 years give or take, which goes by quickly.

I was Jeanie and as much as we are one, I understand that was Jeanie's life as Marilyn not my own. Marilyn Monroe was Norma Jean Baker and although part of her soul lives in me; I am not her. This time around and only this time around I am Mona Lisa Carr Coburn. That's it. I am awakening to all my past lives and perhaps as a fourth-dimensional being I'll be able to remember all of them and what I've learned so I don't have to start at the very beginning again.

Wouldn't it be nice to not make all the same mistakes we've already made? Make wiser decisions, be better at parenting, and so forth. I see the lessons in my past mistakes and as I grow wiser, I'm learning I can give thanks for the lessons. Still, it would be sweet to have past knowledge ready at ones fingertips so we're not starting from scratch.

I hear that is the way some children are now being born, remembering past lives. Good for them, not having to start at the get go, but having a hurdle or two already removed from the track. Not having to learn the hard way that God lives within and is there to help us if we dare ask. Love won't give up on us, it is us that gives up on us. I'd like to know that I have all the confidence in the world to believe in me. God does, Source within does, Angels do, so why not me!

A soft whisper says that is your challenge in life…your worthiness. You brought it forward from your past life, now that you realize it, time to change that belief. Reset, rest in the knowing that all works for the greater good, that angels have your back, that you are a child of the great one true source and are equally worthy and thus capable of having all the confidence you desire for the same creator that brought you forth has brought all beings forth, and ALL are EQUAL.

You are One. The One is the ALL. Never forget the wisdom of the child that lives and abides in you.

You are now awakened and your mission is now to *be* the Light In The World by being you. Sit on a bench and let your light shine. Let your light shine by your mere existence. Your love, your light is needed. Maybe you can't see the invisible waves of love-light, light-love but they do exist. Change the world by sending out your personal waves of light, love. It is more needed than you might come to know. Trust us, trust spirit.

Spirit descends back into All, the One.

Download ✾ 16
Source
June 21

Dearest Great Grandfather Yeshua and All Beings,

Thank you for the brief note on what to write about today. I heard as I woke up; 'Write about the first time you experienced the voice of Source.'

Back In 1996 when my sister Toodie (Naomi) had passed into spirit, after about two months when I laid to go to bed, I thought my dreams had been blocked and I wondered why. I might have even mentioned it aloud to my husband. As I slept, I felt a brilliant bright light come to me. I knew without a doubt that I was in the presence of God. It was an overwhelming feeling of knowing and feeling of love. I was surrounded in a dream state by brilliant light.

As I faced the direction of what I perceived the direction of the source of light, I asked, "Why did you take my dreams from me?"

God/Source said, "To protect you." I instantly knew it was to protect me from my grief over the death of my sister. Not just grief, but depression, despair, guilt of me not being able to help my sister more as she collapsed in multi-diseases and aliments that took her life at just 44 years of age.

"I just wanted to make her happy," I spoke knowing God would know exactly what I meant, and I was speaking of my sister.

"Not your job," Source responded in that instant I knew he meant it was not one's job to make another happy. It was God/Source within that happiness comes from. It was a complete knowing; a truth that can and does transcend one from not believing to believing.

Spirit/God left, and the quickness of the light beam disappearing woke me gasping for my breath and my husband woke seeing a brilliant flash of light zip out through the ceiling. I told him what had just happened in the dream state and with his physical eyes he saw the light beam dash from me out into the cosmos let's say. Also, whenever I have told or written about this story, I have never accurately described the Oneness, the depth of compassion, and love I felt in those brief moments.

It is the feeling of love, compassion, and oneness I now feel when I write with my inner being or guided by spirit, angels, or ascended masters. It's all love, it's all compassion, it feels like truth. Maybe it's only my truth, but it cuts so true as I write these words, I often weep as the depth of love, the depth one wholeness it brings, and the flow oneness. I am not alone. You are not alone.

The thing we've been looking for all our lives, and for many of us in our formative years we found at church, but when we left the church on Sunday mornings it waned, which was spirit saying hey we are real, you are real, and you are spirit too. It's not them or us. It is us, we are one, we are spirits living in a body, living breathing this Heaven on Earth. Earth is Heaven you know. You may choose to see the heartache or choose to see paradise. You are free to choose. I see paradise as it's a lot more fun. Yes, at times my toe dips back into the news which reminds who is doing the unspeakable today. I honestly purposely choose not to listen to it for the most part because I don't want that icky negativity in my reality. I want a clear, high vibration so that I may receive accurate vibrations from the All. Higher I go, clearer I see and the more I realize there is to see.

Peace be to you. Thank you spirit for your words and your wisdom today.

Mona Lisa

Download ✿ 17
Gift of Intuition
June 22

Good morning all Source, Great Grandfather Yeshua, Spirit, and Beings! How are you today? Fantastic and so am I. Thank you for the innate knowing of what to write today.

Yesterday I wrote of the message from Source after my sister's passing. Today I will write of the message I received from my sister after she had been gone for three to four months. Please note I have written it several times and each time it comes out slightly different, but it's always the same message. Today I will let my higher self-guide my words. The experience is as follows:

I was driving along a curvy road in a minivan at that time. Heather, my youngest of three years old was in the child seat in the front passenger seat (Legal at that time). I heard my sister say, "Slow down." I saw her in my third eye. She looked lovely and well! At that time, I didn't understand what the third eye meant and I would describe it as seeing her in the air out the dash window.

I was so struck at what I saw and heard that out loud I said, "What did you say?"

I heard again, plainly and clearly, "Slow down and mom needs you too."

So, if spirit tells you to slow down, one slows down. I did. I was driving with only my right hand on the steering wheel, so I put both hands on the wheel wondering if a deer or another car was right around the next bend. To my surprise as I turned the next bend, Heather, with her car seat and all came flying out of the passenger seat and hit my right arm. If I had been driving with only my right arm, I don't want to imagine what could have happened! It didn't

59

thanks to Spirit. Thanks to my sister for watching out for me! I safely pulled over and secured the child seat back into position and went on my way.

Was it real? Did that really just happen? These are the thoughts that I wrestled with for the remainder of the day. I did not check on my mom when I arrived home. I did not sleep well that night. Uncharacteristically of me I called my mom at 7am the next morning as I was waking the children to get ready for school.

I asked, "Mom how are you?" I will never ever forget her words. "Funny you ask, today I'm alright, but all day yesterday I cried missing your sister."

I humbly told her the story and she cried, "Thank you, thank you. I can't tell you how much that means to me. I've been praying and praying for a sign, and it was given to you."

Today I forgive myself for not accepting spirit in the moment. Why do we doubt spirit? Let me fill with love and the knowing of spirit. Let me follow spirit into the depths of the unknown. Let me know the path spirit wants me to take and let me dive, deep and full of knowing that I'm on the journey to discovering my alchemist.

Today let my soul know that spirit knows the way, that spirit, our inner being often come as intuitiveness in that small wee voice in us that says go this way or do this or don't do that. If we listen to that feeling from our higher selves, we may not win the lottery, but we may live to a better way of life, we may live! What a gift to live and breathe! We may learn that love is all that we are the beggar, we are the millionaire, we are the reflection of all that is around us. All is one and one is all.

Let my writings be of, from spirit and true.

Mona Lisa Coburn

Download ✸ 18
CHRISTMAS EVERY DAY?
June 23

Today is my sister's Toodie's birthday! Happy 71 first birthday! It seems like yesterday you were 44 when you transitioned to the spirit world!

You might have been born with a mental challenge and or when you fell off the monkey bars at 5 years old it might have caused damage too. Either way, life was not easy for you. You rarely ever complained, except with pain as you got older. Your neck hurt, your back hurt. There was little if nothing the doctors at that time could do. Mom was at a loss.

You always offered a bright warm smile to the world, hugs and love. You gave all you could, every dime in your pocket to me or to anyone you that crossed your path. You flowed loved! You were love, pure love. I remember you babysitting the other babies in the family, endlessly, tirelessly. I remember you singing me lullabies and the ABC's. Thank you, there aren't enough thanks for me to give to you.

I remember us visiting the graves of our loved ones and you taught me to say, "I'll see you when we meet again." No truer words were ever spoken. No wiser words were ever given.

You had so many disadvantages like not being able to read in addition to all the physical elements and at the last....so many diseases. At your funeral the rooms were full, standing room only for the one who offered love. That was all you had to give, and you gave it well.

I miss you; I miss the brownies you made, I really miss the chocolate fudge you would whip up every week or so. I miss the homemade ice cream, I miss you!!! We will speak again. I turn on the candle with my third eye and I ask spirit to come to me, in me. Toodie are you there? Are you there for me?

"Yeah, I'm right here. Can you see me?"

I stop and say a short prayer to open up. "My grief is such that I cannot see you. May you speak or write through me? I give you the pen as they say."

Okay, this is the way it is. You allow us to come, and we will come. It's that simple. It is not complicated. One must believe that it is so, and it is so. I love you and I will always be near if you call on me. I'm enjoying Heaven. It's fun. Tell my twin, Happy Birthday Old Man! He's old. I'm not. I am not broken either. It was the plan all along. I taught you compassion and love. Not bad for a spiritual being! Your words touch others, you must believe, and it is so. Mom is beside me and sends her love.

"Hi Pumpkin! All is well."

I hear laughter in my third eye.

"See," Toodie says. *"All is well. Why are you in such a hurry? Do not hurry. Enjoy the swim. Enjoy Vyvyan! Enjoy your friends, and love too. That is life. You are blessed to be here. It's like Christmas down there every day if you let it. Can you let it? Can you let the flowers, the animals, the sun, the water be gifts to cheer your heart, to warm your soul and feel Christmas every day?"*

"If you want to know the secret to life, I just gave it to you. Your other versions of your soul gave it to you. Live now, follow your passion, love, enjoy even the pain, and it won't be pain anymore. Life is better than good; life is a great big gift. Life is the best present of all. Is it now? You don't know what tomorrow will bring? Just like you don't know what is in that gift box. Remember what a

joy it is to unfold. Remember that is how children look at it. It is astounding how many lost their way. I'm so proud of you! You have taught me that there is joy in discovering ones higher self. How high can you climb? I will be with you, your guides are with you, angels are with you. You do not walk alone. Remember your faith? Yes, you lost it once due to man's teachings. Now you see Great Grandfather was a man who had children! He whispered in your ear I do not want to be worshiped. I want you to see All in You and One in All. We feel that you have had glimpses and you are on your way."

"We offer you love and support to follow your heart, to follow your path, we are there, here with you in spirit. You have opened the door. Walk, run, climb up those spiritual steps. It's so fun to see you grow. You grow all of you at your own rate. You are growing and growing. I see you. I'm learning from you. You are more than you could ever imagine. You got this! I love you. Thank you for your love. Thank you for your appreciation for me. It warms us on this side.

Be happy, be at peace. Frosty is Roscoe. He came a long way to be with you. Isn't that grand! You are so very loved.

I'm with Hope. Do not cry my sister for we will be together again as souls that unite. Don't ever forget I am with you in spirit.

"I'll see you when you get here! Now go make some fudge!

Toodie, Naomi Alver McAlpin.

Download ✦ 19
Message from Spirit Guides
June 26

Dearest Spirit,

"Do you have anything to say? I, Mona Lisa ask telepathically as I take a deep breath. I breathe in Source and breathe out love."

I hear the following as I type with my eyes semi closed:

> *"It is time to put paper to print. Those who are awakened need to know that being alive pulls up the positive energy here on this planet and lets love, light flourish more and more. Positive energy vibrates out and seeks its own, multiplying its radiance."*

> *"On final words of thought for your readers we your spirit guides want them to know that your messages came from and us, and yes some were through spiritual masters, spirits, angels, and consciousness whom Mona Lisa's interpretation is close to 90% accuracy. She is not perfect, and these messages are purposely designed that way. She is the great daughter of Yeshua, and we did not want her word/words to be or have any type of religious connotation. They are from spirit to you and to those with open hearts that are willing to hear clear honest messages and not get hung up on a word or two."*

> *"For those who are awakened and understand the words; I am that I am, try to understand this; the world needs you more than ever HERE. Right here. Be you, your awakened self, be you at play, be you in stillness and send out your love, your*

*peace to the world. The world, the Universe will,
and does shine brighter when you do."*

*"Once again if you're awakened and wondering
'now what;' we encourage you to stay and be; be
you the best you can be, rejoice in the knowing,
the knowledge that the spirit world is here to
support you. Listen and be content in the
acknowledgement you are loved, so very loved
and eternal. Now you need to be the LIGHT, to
be the LOVE so that planet earth continues its
beautiful upward spiral to awaken positive
universal presence."*

*What can you do? Like Mona Lisa was trying to
say with her words: educate, meditate,
appreciate, and radiate. What does that mean
learn and continue on your self-awaken path as
that is the only true way. Meditation is one way to
continue to grow as a spiritual being. In
appreciation for all that is like another day on this
spinning ball and all that you have is
fundamental in joy and love. It's living in the
now. Radiate by send love and peace whenever
you can. As you go for walks, as you go for car
rides, as you go anywhere, and or nowhere send
out love. It may be a smile, a friendly nod, kind
words or deeds, but it doesn't have to be. You can
close your eyes and concentrate on sending out
love and so it is.*

*"Follow your heart, follow your joy and watch the
world change directly before your eyes. See the
good in all. Lastly know without the negative you
would not know what the positive looks or feels
like. Rejoice in all things. Allow life to unfold
with nonjudgement and rest in the being you.*

Remember nonjudgement is with an 'AND' not 'OR.' It's Them and Me. Good and Bad. Light and Dark. For how can one see the light without the darkness?"

"Who am I? I am the consciousness of Mona Lisa's spirit guides. You can find a glimpse of us in her novels. The characters of some of her hero's and spirit guides such as Xelas, Dajoji, and Nibi are from the inspiration we gave her and some of those traits we do possess."

I don't think it gets simpler than that.

In love, in spirit, Mona Lisa's Spirit Guides: aka Xelas, Dajoji, and Nibi.

Download ✸ 20
HOW TO RAISE YOUR FREQUENCY
June 29

Things to practice:

1. Say, "I am that I am" until it feels like home. Until you know what it means to your truth. Literally sit with it, close your eyes and practice saying it. You might also want to say another version of it like, "Who am I?"

2. Finish these thoughts: I am happiest when_____.
   I am also happy when I_____.
   Write down all the things that make you happy, for they lift your vibrations! How high can you go?

3. Today I will take time to breathe and send out love in the following ways:

   a.

   b.

   c.

   d.

   e.

Things that can help a vibration to raise are doing things that promote joy for you, service work, and meditation. Going for walks, exercise, playing with pets, hot baths are a few ways I like to bring up my vibration. I love doing at least a few of these every day. What brings you peace? What brings you joy?

What to take away from this reading:

Create: You are source in a body; express your joy that is why you're here.

Educate: Continue to learn following your truth on your awakened path. Be your own Hero first.

Meditate: It naturally allows you to take time out for you and one learns the art of allowing.

Appreciate: Now is all we have and now and now and now. Live in the moment especially with play and love.

Radiate: Toss good vibes around like rose petals, send your light on to the planet to raise every vibration.

I hope you allow yourself to participate in as many ways you can daily to embrace your own self awakening path.

In love and service.

MonaLisa

Download ✪ 21
CELEBRATE YOU!
June 30

Dearest Great Grandfather Yeshua or any spiritual beings,

"I come in humble service Do you have any parting words for the reader as I close this book?"

"The planet no longer is in third density. It now vibrates at 4ᵗʰ density. This is an exciting time on this planet. If you are here, right now that means that you planned it. That means that the children being born are born into a naturally higher vibration."

"This is the time that the entire Universe is watching planet Earth. While there are so many other conscious species none have gone through exactly like what the earth is going through. Yes, species awaken to know that they are eternal souls, but each has taken their own unique path. Earth's path is not an easy school. It's like graduation class, this Earth school. This is a time of celebration. Celebrate who you are and where you are on your path."

"Rejoice in the knowing, the knowledge your soul lives forever!"

"Be the creator of your life and color it how you wish knowing source is supporting you and loving you always."

Peace to you.

Xelas,
Spirit Guide

Download ✹ 22
YESHUA: LIVE IN THE ETERNAL NOW
July 1

Download from my walk in the forest this morning:

"Good morning Grandfather!"

"Good morning Mona Lisa."

"Do you have anything else you would like to say? Like I was wondering what were your real teachings when you were alive?"

"I can tell you some, but know that they were from Source as I understood it in a human body:

"I was teaching that All is One and the One is All in the sense that I was trying to get the masses to see that women and men are equal in the Creator's eye. That man needs woman to survive, and woman needs man to survive. Remember the story of the children? Least harm one of them, you do the same to me? I was trying to show people that children are equal in the eyes of the Creator and needed to be honored as such."

"Those teachings are relevant today that we are each a reflection of the creator. We each have God within us. We each our creators of our reality, our own truth. The God within us, is the Me, it's your higher self, it's the open door to all that is where possibilities are endless and love springs eternal."

"Remember my child, it's all about unconditional love for yourself, for others, and allowance. Allow angels, spirit guides, and all on this side to guide

you, to support you and lift you up. No-one ever walks alone. Everyone sooner or later always goes to Heaven, even those who believe in Hell and go there. At some point they think of Heaven and are there. They may not like the idea of their life review, but remember it is without judgement. It is for the learning of the soul. Spirit world is your home world. Life on earth is precious and goes by so very quickly, like the blink of an eye and it's over. Enjoy every second that you can, love every second that you can, be of service every second that you can, be nonjudgmental with a full unconditional loving heart. Never forget it takes the darkness to see the light. These are keys to a good joyful life, not one without grief or pain. Pain is a part of life, suffering or choosing to focus on the loss and or pain is suffering."

Need help? Ask your spirit guides, ask your angels, ask! We are here to assist you always.

Now go and live, live in the eternal now.

In love and service your Great Grand Father,

Yeshua.

July 1, 2023

Bibliography

(Editor), Marvin Meyer. 2007. *The Nag Hammadi Scriptures.* HarperOne.

Channeling, One Consciousness, interview by MonaLisa Coburn. 2023. (June).

n.d. *Family Search.* Accessed July 3, 2023. https://www.familysearch.org/en/.

n.d. "Genealogy of Jesus and Mary." *Priory of Sion.* Accessed August 20, 2023. http://www.prieure-de-sion.com/4/genealogy_of_jesus_and_mary_860930.html.

Greer, Dr. Steven. 2023. "UFO Whistleblower Conference." Washington, DC.

Leloup, Jean-Yves. 2002. *The Gospel of Mary Magdalene.* Rochester, VT: Inner Traditions.

Watkins, Donald V. n.d. "The Royal Bloodline: The Descendants of Jesus and Mary Magdalene." Accessed August 20, 2023. https://www.donaldwatkins.com/post/the-royal-bloodline-the-descendants-of-jesus-and-mary-magdalene.

Wolter, Scott F. 2019. *Cryptic Code of the Templars in America.* North Star Press.

ABOUT THE AUTHOR

MonaLisa's passion is teaching about One Consciousness and does so by public speaking engagements, through her books, YouTube channel and offering intuitive services and life guidance on her web site.

MonaLisa Coburn was born in California and still resides there with her husband Charlie of over 40 years. They live near the forest with their two dogs, Roscoe and Amba. MonaLisa has three grown children and loves to write. She has always loved to write, and through the years she has written many books and slowly is awakening to allow them to be published.

MonaLisa's Dream Navigators series of novels has been inspired by spirit guides and is being edited and published. At the time of writing the Dream Navigators novels, MonaLisa didn't understand that these stories being brought to her in her dreams were actually channeling events directly from spirit. Over the years since writing them she has discovered more truths in the stories than she even imagined!

Other Titles by MonaLisa:
Dream Navigators 1: The Dawn of Nahee
Dream Navigators 2: The Christening by Fire
Dream Navigators 3 through 5 (comming soon).
Universal Toolbox

www.ChannelingOC.com

Made in the USA
Middletown, DE
13 December 2024

66999813R00049